COMPANION STUDY GUIDE

BECAUSE OF WHO *YOU* ARE

THE STORIES BEHIND MY MUSIC

MARTHA MUNIZZI

Copyright © 2023 by Martha Munizzi

Published by Arrows & Stones

All rights reserved. No portion of this book may be reproduced, stored in a retrieval system, or transmitted in any form or by any means—electronic, mechanical, photocopy, recording, scanning, or other—except for brief quotations in critical reviews or articles, without prior written permission of the author.

For foreign and subsidiary rights, contact the author.

Cover design by: Sara Young
Cover photo by: STYLZ (front cover), Ashley Mae Wright (back cover)

ISBN: 978-1-957369-18-1   1 2 3 4 5 6 7 8 9 10

Printed in the United States of America

BECAUSE OF WHO *YOU ARE*

THE STORIES BEHIND MY MUSIC

MARTHA MUNIZZI

CONTENTS

INTRODUCTION 6
1. BECAUSE OF WHO YOU ARE 8
2. 'TIL THE WALLS FALL 12
3. I'M GONNA WIN 18
4. WORTHY 22
5. NEW SEASON 28
6. GRATEFUL 32
7. HOLY SPIRIT, FILL THIS ROOM 36
8. RENEW ME 42
9. I KNOW THE PLANS 46
10. MAKE IT LOUD 52
11. SAY THE NAME 56
12. WE SAY YES 64
13. HEAVEN 70
14. SHOUT 74
15. THE GREAT EXCHANGE 80
16. HE'S ALREADY PROVIDED 84
17. GLORIOUS 90
18. MY STRENGTH 94
19. NO CONDEMNATION 102
20. YOU'VE BEEN SO GOOD 106
21. ASK 110
22. COME, HOLY SPIRIT, COME 116
23. DECLARATION SONG
    (DECLARE THE GOODNESS OF OUR GOD) 124
24. FIGHT FOR ME 132
25. LIFT HIM UP 138
26. YOUR LATTER WILL BE GREATER 142
27. JESUS IS THE BEST THING
    (THAT EVER HAPPENED TO ME) 146
28. BEST DAYS 150
29. EVERYTHING YOU DO IS A BLESSING 154
30. GOD IS HERE 158

INTRODUCTION

Hopefully, you already have a copy of *Because of Who You Are: The Stories Behind My Music* –I wrote this book to tell the stories behind the writing of thirty of some of my most popular worship songs. This companion journal was created to let you write down, reflect on, and pray about the content from the book.

Take time to think about what you read in *Because of Who You Are* and write down any thoughts and insights you have. Listen to what the Lord may be trying to say to you through the stories and the lyrics of my songs. I pray that through this book and your time spent journaling and reflecting, you'll be encouraged, empowered, and inspired in your walk with the Lord.

THE SOAP DEVOTIONAL PROCESS: S.O.A.P.

S.O.A.P. stands for Scripture, Observation, Application, and Prayer. By utilizing the SOAP method, we can be more intentional and learn more from God's Living Word. To use the SOAP method, just focus on these four key areas in your journaling:

SCRIPTURE

Write down the scripture that catches your eye (and heart) as you read your Bible each day. Which verses does the Holy Spirit want you to take a second look at?

OBSERVATION

Take time to research and think on the context of the verses you have selected. Who or what are they referring to? Who are they written by?

APPLICATION

What is the application of the selected verse(s)? Think about how the verse applies to your current situation and environment and how you can use what is in the verse on what is ahead.

PRAYER

Write and pray a prayer to God that includes what you've learned and ask Him to apply the truths of His Word in your life.

CHAPTER 1

BECAUSE OF WHO YOU ARE

"Because of who You are, I give You glory. . . ."

READING TIME

As you read Chapter 1: "Because Of Who You Are" in *Because of Who You Are*, review, reflect on, and respond to the text by answering the following questions.

REVIEW, REFLECT, AND RESPOND

Of God's names, how has He revealed Himself to you recently? Explain your answer.

_____
_____
_____
_____

Who is God to you? How has your perception of God's identity changed over the years?

_____
_____
_____

How do you worship the Lord for who He is in your daily life? What needs to change for you to focus more on Him?

_____
_____
_____
_____

What stands out to you from the lyrics of this song and why? What do these lyrics mean to you?

_____
_____
_____
_____

READINGS: PHILIPPIANS 4

S:

O:

A:

P:

S.O.A.P.

SCRIPTURE

Write down the scripture that catches your eye (and heart) as you read your Bible each day. Which verses does the Holy Spirit want you to take a second look at?

OBSERVATION

Take time to research and think on the context of the verses you have selected. Who or what are they referring to? Who are they written by?

APPLICATION

What is the application of the selected verse(s)? Think about how the verse applies to your current situation and environment and how you can use what is in the verse on what is ahead.

PRAYER

Write and pray a prayer to God that includes what you've learned and ask Him to apply the truths of His Word in your life.

CHAPTER 2
"'TIL THE WALLS FALL"

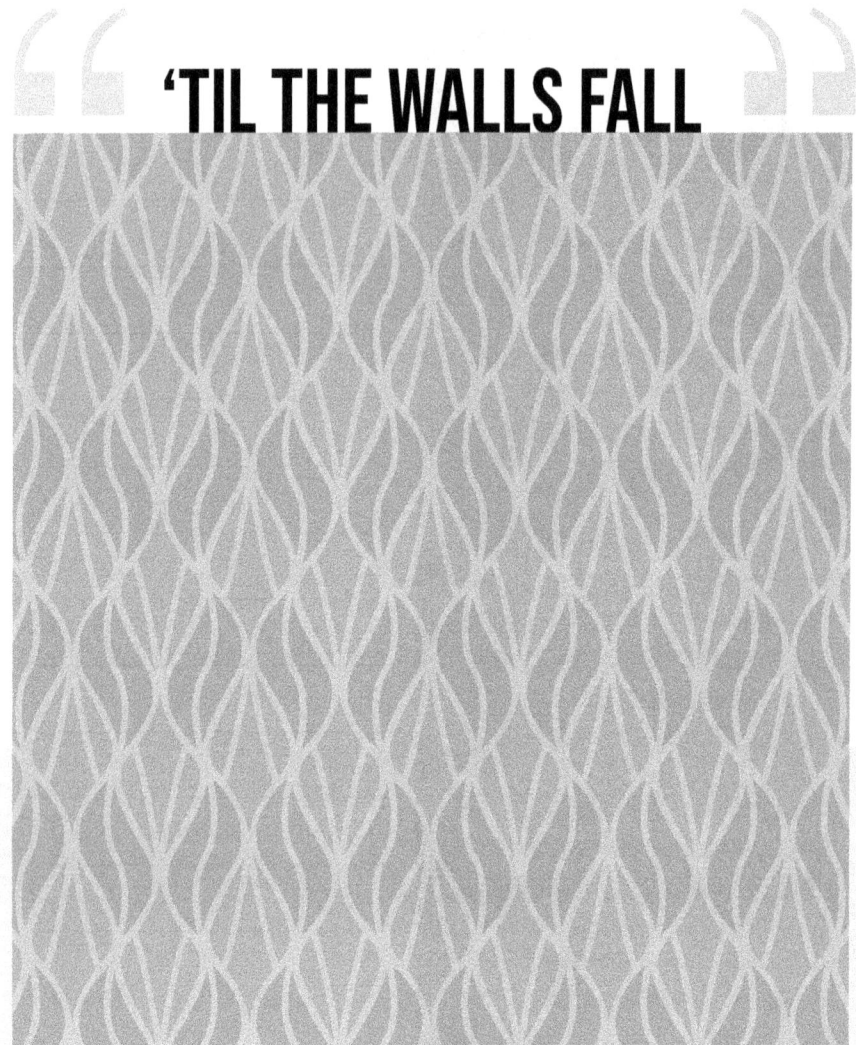

♪

*"Praise until the walls fall
Praise until the enemy's under my feet...."*

READING TIME

As you read Chapter 2: "'Til The Walls Fall" in *Because of Who You Are*, review, reflect on, and respond to the text by answering the following questions.

REVIEW, REFLECT, AND RESPOND

In your own words, what does it mean to praise, "until the walls fall"?

_____
_____
_____

What do you feel the walls in this song represent?

_____
_____
_____
_____

What is one circumstance from your past God has helped you overcome? What is one situation you're currently facing that you need His help with?

_____
_____
_____
_____

What stands out to you from the lyrics of this song and why? What do these lyrics mean to you?

_____
_____
_____
_____

READINGS: DEUTERONOMY 7

S:

O:

A:

P:

JOSHUA 6

S:

O:

A:

P:

HEBREWS 11:30

S:

O:

A:

P:

PHILIPPIANS 1:6

S:

O:

A:

P:

CHAPTER 3

I'M GONNA WIN

♪

*"I'm gonna win'
'Cause God says so...."*

READING TIME

As you read Chapter 3: "I'm Gonna Win" in *Because of Who You Are*, review, reflect on, and respond to the text by answering the following questions.

REVIEW, REFLECT, AND RESPOND

How would you define "winning" in the context of this song? What does it look like to win?

_____

_____

_____

_____

Why is it important to keep moving forward despite what things may look like?

_____

_____

_____

_____

Do you think winning is a journey or a destination? How do you feel the world's definition of winning differs from that of God's?

_____

_____

_____

_____

What stands out to you from the lyrics of this song and why? What do these lyrics mean to you?

_____

_____

_____

_____

READINGS: 2 CORINTHIANS 2

S:

O:

A:

P:

S.O.A.P.

SCRIPTURE

Write down the scripture that catches your eye (and heart) as you read your Bible each day. Which verses does the Holy Spirit want you to take a second look at?

OBSERVATION

Take time to research and think on the context of the verses you have selected. Who or what are they referring to? Who are they written by?

APPLICATION

What is the application of the selected verse(s)? Think about how the verse applies to your current situation and environment and how you can use what is in the verse on what is ahead.

PRAYER

Write and pray a prayer to God that includes what you've learned and ask Him to apply the truths of His Word in your life.

CHAPTER 4

WORTHY

♪

*"Worthy of all the glory
Worthy of all the praise. . . ."*

READING TIME

As you read Chapter 4: "Worthy" in *Because of Who You Are*, **review, reflect on, and respond to** the text by answering the following questions.

REVIEW, REFLECT, AND RESPOND

What do you feel makes God worthy of all the glory and praise?

_____
_____
_____
_____

How can we live out the command of 1 Thessalonians 5:18 and give thanks in every situation?

_____
_____
_____
_____

In what ways can we give God glory and praise?

_____
_____
_____
_____

What stands out to you from the lyrics of this song and why? What do these lyrics mean to you?

_____
_____
_____
_____

READINGS: 1 THESSALONIANS 5

S:

O:

A:

P:

♪

JOB 8:21

S:

O:

A:

P:

PROVERBS 31:25

S:

O:

A:

P:

♪

JOHN 11:41

S:

O:

A:

P:

CHAPTER 5

NEW SEASON

♪

"It's all available to you right now just taste and see; it's a new season. . . ."

READING TIME

As you read Chapter 5: "New Season" in *Because of Who You Are*, review, reflect on, and respond to the text by answering the following questions.

REVIEW, REFLECT, AND RESPOND

How does God use the different seasons in our life to prepare us for what is ahead?

_____
_____
_____
_____

What season of life are you currently in? What do you feel you need to work on most in this present season?

_____
_____
_____
_____

Describe a period in your life where seasons changed when you weren't expecting it. What happened? What did you learn?

_____
_____
_____
_____

What stands out to you from the lyrics of this song and why? What do these lyrics mean to you?

_____
_____
_____
_____

READINGS: ECCLESIASTES 3

S:

O:

A:

P:

S.O.A.P.

SCRIPTURE

Write down the scripture that catches your eye (and heart) as you read your Bible each day. Which verses does the Holy Spirit want you to take a second look at?

OBSERVATION

Take time to research and think on the context of the verses you have selected. Who or what are they referring to? Who are they written by?

APPLICATION

What is the application of the selected verse(s)? Think about how the verse applies to your current situation and environment and how you can use what is in the verse on what is ahead.

PRAYER

Write and pray a prayer to God that includes what you've learned and ask Him to apply the truths of His Word in your life.

CHAPTER 6

"GRATEFUL"

♪

*"What can I say
But 'Thank You, Jesus'?..."*

READING TIME

As you read Chapter 6: "Grateful" in *Because of Who You Are*, **review, reflect on, and respond to the text by answering the following questions.**

REVIEW, REFLECT, AND RESPOND

Are you grateful for all that God has done in your life, seen and unseen? How do you communicate this gratitude to Him?

_____
_____
_____

What are you most grateful to God for? Would you still be thankful even if He took this away?

_____
_____
_____

What area or areas of your life have you not shown gratitude to the Lord in? Take time to think on how He has blessed you in these areas, even if it is not immediately evident.

_____
_____
_____
_____

What stands out to you from the lyrics of this song and why? What do these lyrics mean to you?

_____
_____
_____
_____

READINGS:
1 THESSALONIANS 5:18

S:

O:

A:

P:

1 THESSALONIANS 6

S:

O:

A:

P:

CHAPTER 7

HOLY SPIRIT, FILL THIS ROOM

♪

"We need Your presence—we need You. . . ."

READING TIME

As you read Chapter 7: "Holy Spirit, Fill This Room" in *Because of Who You Are*, review, reflect on, and respond to the text by answering the following questions.

REVIEW, REFLECT, AND RESPOND

How would you describe the presence of the Holy Spirit to a nonbeliever?

_____
_____
_____
_____

In your own words, what is the power and purpose of the Holy Spirit?

_____
_____
_____

What are you harboring in your life that may be inhibiting the Holy Spirit from guiding you? Worry? Doubt? Fear? Take time to introspect and identify any bad habits or mindsets.

_____
_____
_____
_____

What stands out to you from the lyrics of this song and why? What do these lyrics mean to you?

_____
_____
_____
_____

READINGS: EXODUS 13

S:

O:

A:

P:

1 CORINTHIANS 2:9-11

S:

O:

A:

P:

♪

ZECHARIAH 4:6

S:

O:

A:

P:

PHILIPPIANS 4:6-7

S:

O:

A:

P:

CHAPTER 8

RENEW ME

♪

"Renew a right spirit within me. . . ."

READING TIME

As you read Chapter 8: "Renew Me" in *Because of Who You Are*, **review, reflect on, and respond to** the text by answering the following questions.

REVIEW, REFLECT, AND RESPOND

What does it mean to "renew" the spirit within someone?

_____
_____
_____
_____

How often do you renew your heart? How do you go about making it clean?

_____
_____
_____
_____

Do you think the renewing of our hearts is an event or a process? Explain your answer.

_____
_____
_____
_____

What stands out to you from the lyrics of this song and why? What do these lyrics mean to you?

_____
_____
_____
_____

READINGS: PSALM 51

S:

O:

A:

P:

S.O.A.P.

SCRIPTURE

Write down the scripture that catches your eye (and heart) as you read your Bible each day. Which verses does the Holy Spirit want you to take a second look at?

OBSERVATION

Take time to research and think on the context of the verses you have selected. Who or what are they referring to? Who are they written by?

APPLICATION

What is the application of the selected verse(s)? Think about how the verse applies to your current situation and environment and how you can use what is in the verse on what is ahead.

PRAYER

Write and pray a prayer to God that includes what you've learned and ask Him to apply the truths of His Word in your life.

CHAPTER 9

"I KNOW THE PLANS"

♪

*"Remember, I know
the plans I have for you...."*

READING TIME

As you read Chapter 9: "I Know The Plans" in *Because of Who You Are*, review, reflect on, and respond to the text by answering the following questions.

REVIEW, REFLECT, AND RESPOND

Do you believe God has plans for your life? How has God blessed you beyond what you dreamed or imagined in the past?

_____
_____
_____
_____

Have you ever tried to put your life plans above God's plans for your life? What was the outcome?

_____
_____
_____
_____

What do you put your hope in day-to-day? Is it entirely in God, or something else?

_____
_____
_____
_____

What stands out to you from the lyrics of this song and why? What do these lyrics mean to you?

_____
_____
_____
_____

READINGS: JEREMIAH 29

S:

O:

A:

P:

EPHESIANS 2:10

S: _____

O: _____

A: _____

P: _____

♪

HEBREWS 11:1

S:

O:

A:

P:

♪

ISAIAH 40:31

S: _____

_____

_____

_____

O: _____

_____

_____

_____

A: _____

_____

_____

_____

P: _____

_____

_____

_____

CHAPTER 10

"MAKE IT LOUD"

♪

*"All around the world
Celebrate Jesus! . . ."*

READING TIME

As you read Chapter 10: "Make It Loud" in *Because of Who You Are*, review, reflect on, and respond to the text by answering the following questions.

REVIEW, REFLECT, AND RESPOND

How do you celebrate Jesus before others? Have you ever been ashamed or embarrassed of your passion for your Lord and Savior?

_____
_____
_____
_____

Do you ever have trouble focusing on what God is doing instead of what the enemy's scheme is? Why do you think this is?

_____
_____
_____

Have you ever amped up your praise and worship in the midst of seemingly dire circumstances? What happened? Describe the situation.

_____
_____
_____

What stands out to you from the lyrics of this song and why? What do these lyrics mean to you?

_____
_____
_____

READINGS: EXODUS 15

S:

O:

A:

P:

♪

2 CHRONICLES 20:22

S:

O:

A:

P:

CHAPTER 11

SAY THE NAME

♪

*"When you don't know what else to say
Say the name...."*

READING TIME

As you read Chapter 11: "Say The Name" in *Because of Who You Are*, review, reflect on, and respond to the text by answering the following questions.

REVIEW, REFLECT, AND RESPOND

Have any of your battles turned out to be blessings? Why is it so hard to see the good part of difficulty in the midst of it?

_____
_____
_____
_____

In your own words, how would you describe the power that is in the name of Jesus Christ?

_____
_____
_____
_____

Do you say Jesus' name in your life? When do you use it?

_____
_____
_____
_____

What stands out to you from the lyrics of this song and why? What do these lyrics mean to you?

_____
_____
_____

READINGS: MARK 16

S:

O:

A:

P:

♪

MATTHEW 28:18

S:

O:

A:

P:

♪

PHILIPPIANS 2:9-10

S:

O:

A:

P:

♪

PROVERBS 18:10

S:

O:

A:

P:

PSALM 34:7

S:

O:

A:

P:

S.O.A.P.

SCRIPTURE

Write down the scripture that catches your eye (and heart) as you read your Bible each day. Which verses does the Holy Spirit want you to take a second look at?

OBSERVATION

Take time to research and think on the context of the verses you have selected. Who or what are they referring to? Who are they written by?

APPLICATION

What is the application of the selected verse(s)? Think about how the verse applies to your current situation and environment and how you can use what is in the verse on what is ahead.

PRAYER

Write and pray a prayer to God that includes what you've learned and ask Him to apply the truths of His Word in your life.

CHAPTER 12

WE SAY YES

♪

*"We say yes
Yes to every miracle
Yes to the supernatural...."*

READING TIME

As you read Chapter 12 "We Say Yes" in *Because of Who You Are*, **review, reflect on, and respond to the text by answering the following questions.**

REVIEW, REFLECT, AND RESPOND

Do you ever have trouble doubting that God will do what He said He will do? Why or why not?

_____
_____
_____

Does it take God finishing what He is doing for you to believe? What makes you say yes to God?

_____
_____
_____
_____

In your own words, how would you define faith? Do you have faith? Do you have enough faith?

_____
_____
_____
_____

What stands out to you from the lyrics of this song and why? What do these lyrics mean to you?

_____
_____
_____
_____

READINGS: NUMBERS 13:30

S:

O:

A:

P:

NUMBERS 14

S:

O:

A:

P:

♪

PSALM 37:4

S:

O:

A:

P:

HEBREWS 11:3

S:

O:

A:

P:

CHAPTER 13

HEAVEN

♪

"I wanna see heaven, heaven on earth...."

READING TIME

As you read Chapter 13: "Heaven" in *Because of Who You Are*, **review, reflect on, and respond to** the text by answering the following questions.

REVIEW, REFLECT, AND RESPOND

In your own opinion, what is the best part about heaven? What are you most looking forward to? What does heaven mean to you?

_____
_____
_____
_____

What does it mean to look at things from "heaven's perspective"? What in your life do you need to look at from this perspective?

_____
_____
_____
_____

What can you do each day to bring a little bit of heaven down to earth? Give some realistic action steps.

_____
_____
_____

What stands out to you from the lyrics of this song and why? What do these lyrics mean to you?

_____
_____
_____

READINGS: MATTHEW 6

S:

O:

A:

P:

S.O.A.P.

SCRIPTURE

Write down the scripture that catches your eye (and heart) as you read your Bible each day. Which verses does the Holy Spirit want you to take a second look at?

OBSERVATION

Take time to research and think on the context of the verses you have selected. Who or what are they referring to? Who are they written by?

APPLICATION

What is the application of the selected verse(s)? Think about how the verse applies to your current situation and environment and how you can use what is in the verse on what is ahead.

PRAYER

Write and pray a prayer to God that includes what you've learned and ask Him to apply the truths of His Word in your life.

CHAPTER 14

SHOUT

♪

*"Shout for the victory
Shout if you've been set free...."*

READING TIME

As you read Chapter 14: "Shout" in *Because of Who You Are*, **review, reflect on, and respond to** the text by answering the following questions.

REVIEW, REFLECT, AND RESPOND

What reasons do you have to shout with a voice of triumph, praise, and victory?

_____
_____
_____
_____

Is there power in praise? Why or why not?

_____
_____
_____
_____

Have you ever let the enemy intimidate you and silence your shouts of praise to God? Describe the experience.

_____
_____
_____
_____

What stands out to you from the lyrics of this song and why? What do these lyrics mean to you?

_____
_____
_____
_____

READINGS: PSALM 47

S:

O:

A:

P:

♪

PSALM 8:2

S:

O:

A:

P:

♪

JAMES 4:7

S:

O:

A:

P:

S.O.A.P.

SCRIPTURE

Write down the scripture that catches your eye (and heart) as you read your Bible each day. Which verses does the Holy Spirit want you to take a second look at?

OBSERVATION

Take time to research and think on the context of the verses you have selected. Who or what are they referring to? Who are they written by?

APPLICATION

What is the application of the selected verse(s)? Think about how the verse applies to your current situation and environment and how you can use what is in the verse on what is ahead.

PRAYER

Write and pray a prayer to God that includes what you've learned and ask Him to apply the truths of His Word in your life.

CHAPTER 15

THE GREAT EXCHANGE

♪

"My sin erased—my heart is free! . . ."

READING TIME

As you read Chapter 15: "The Great Exchange" in *Because of Who You Are*, **review, reflect on, and respond to** the text by answering the following questions.

REVIEW, REFLECT, AND RESPOND

What is being "exchanged" when we worship the Lord? What have you surrendered to Him, and what has He replaced it with?

_____
_____
_____
_____

How can we enter into God's holy presence? What does it take on your end? Explain.

_____
_____
_____
_____

How does one trade in "mourning" for "dancing"? What inhibits this process?

_____
_____
_____
_____

What stands out to you from the lyrics of this song and why? What do these lyrics mean to you?

_____
_____
_____
_____

READINGS: PSALM 40

S:

O:

A:

P:

S.O.A.P.

SCRIPTURE

Write down the scripture that catches your eye (and heart) as you read your Bible each day. Which verses does the Holy Spirit want you to take a second look at?

OBSERVATION

Take time to research and think on the context of the verses you have selected. Who or what are they referring to? Who are they written by?

APPLICATION

What is the application of the selected verse(s)? Think about how the verse applies to your current situation and environment and how you can use what is in the verse on what is ahead.

PRAYER

Write and pray a prayer to God that includes what you've learned and ask Him to apply the truths of His Word in your life.

CHAPTER 16

"HE'S ALREADY PROVIDED"

♪

*"Just ask it in His name
'Cause everything you need
He's already provided. . . ."*

READING TIME

As you read Chapter 16: "He's Already Provided" in *Because of Who You Are*, review, reflect on, and respond to the text by answering the following questions.

REVIEW, REFLECT, AND RESPOND

What needs in your life do you find yourself stressing about? Do you think if you stopped stressing, you would still be provided with everything you need? Why or why not?

_____
_____
_____
_____

Which of God's promises discussed in this chapter are you waiting for currently?

_____
_____
_____

What does it mean to possess God's promises by faith? Are you doing this as you wait for Him to fulfill His promise?

_____
_____
_____
_____

What stands out to you from the lyrics of this song and why? What do these lyrics mean to you?

_____
_____
_____

READINGS: 2 PETER 1

S:

O:

A:

P:

EPHESIANS 1:3

S:

O:

A:

P:

PHILIPPIANS 4:19

S:

O:

A:

P:

♪

PSALM 37:23

S:

O:

A:

P:

CHAPTER 17

"GLORIOUS"

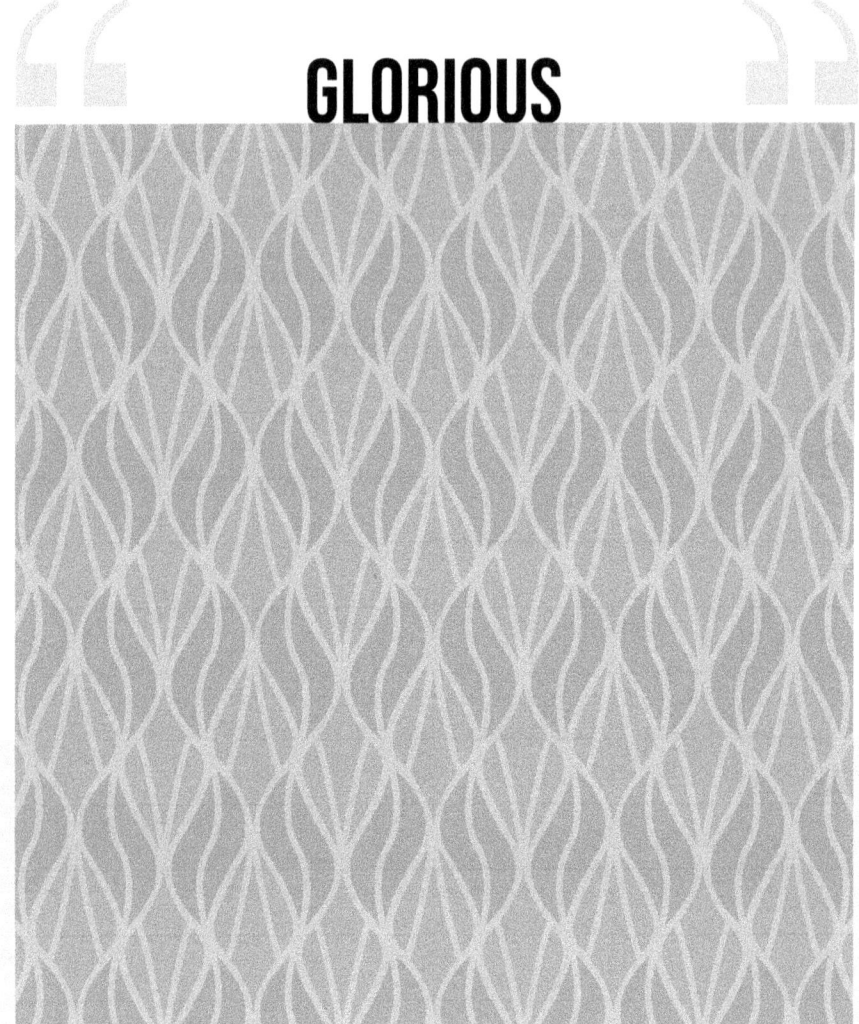

♪

*"Get to shouting, and make it loud
And make His praise glorious, glorious. . . ."*

READING TIME

As you read Chapter 17: "Glorious" in *Because of Who You Are*, **review, reflect on, and respond to the text by answering the following questions.**

REVIEW, REFLECT, AND RESPOND

What do you think God's Word means in Psalm 66 when it says to "make [God's] praise glorious"?

_____
_____
_____

Do you think glorious praise is from the heart, or an external outpouring? Explain your answer.

_____
_____
_____
_____

How does our praise cause the devil to react? Should this be our primary motivation in worship?

_____
_____
_____
_____

What stands out to you from the lyrics of this song and why? What do these lyrics mean to you?

_____
_____
_____
_____

READINGS: PSALM 66

S:

O:

A:

P:

S.O.A.P.

SCRIPTURE

Write down the scripture that catches your eye (and heart) as you read your Bible each day. Which verses does the Holy Spirit want you to take a second look at?

OBSERVATION

Take time to research and think on the context of the verses you have selected. Who or what are they referring to? Who are they written by?

APPLICATION

What is the application of the selected verse(s)? Think about how the verse applies to your current situation and environment and how you can use what is in the verse on what is ahead.

PRAYER

Write and pray a prayer to God that includes what you've learned and ask Him to apply the truths of His Word in your life.

CHAPTER 18

MY STRENGTH

♪

*"O the joy of the Lord is
My strength, my strength...."*

READING TIME

As you read Chapter 18: "My Strength" in *Because of Who You Are*, review, reflect on, and respond to the text by answering the following questions.

REVIEW, REFLECT, AND RESPOND

What are all of the fruits of the Spirit? Which of these fruits do you most need to work on embodying in your life and why?

_____
_____
_____
_____

Why should we work our hardest to embody the fruits of the Spirit in our lives? What good will this do for the kingdom?

_____
_____
_____
_____

How is the joy of the Lord your strength? In what way can this joy strengthen someone?

_____
_____
_____
_____

What stands out to you from the lyrics of this song and why? What do these lyrics mean to you?

_____
_____
_____
_____

READINGS: GALATIANS 5

S:

O:

A:

P:

♪

ISAIAH 61:3

S:

O:

A:

P:

♪

NEHEMIAH 8:10

S:

O:

A:

P:

JOHN 15:11

S:

O:

A:

P:

HEBREWS 12:2

S:

O:

A:

P:

LUKE 15:7

S:

O:

A:

P:

CHAPTER 19

NO CONDEMNATION

♪

*"Because of His forgiveness
I don't have to live with shame anymore...."*

READING TIME

As you read Chapter 19: "No Condemnation" in *Because of Who You Are*, review, reflect on, and respond to the text by answering the following questions.

REVIEW, REFLECT, AND RESPOND

Why is there no place for shame among the children of God? Does God desire for us to be ashamed of what we have and haven't done?

_____
_____
_____
_____

How can fear and self-preservation limit us from all that God has planned? How can we overcome these inhibiting traits?

_____
_____
_____
_____

Are you living free from your sin, shame, and condemnation, or are you letting them slow you down? How can you be sure?

_____
_____
_____
_____

What stands out to you from the lyrics of this song and why? What do these lyrics mean to you?

_____
_____
_____
_____

READINGS: ROMANS 8

S:

O:

A:

P:

S.O.A.P.

SCRIPTURE

Write down the scripture that catches your eye (and heart) as you read your Bible each day. Which verses does the Holy Spirit want you to take a second look at?

OBSERVATION

Take time to research and think on the context of the verses you have selected. Who or what are they referring to? Who are they written by?

APPLICATION

What is the application of the selected verse(s)? Think about how the verse applies to your current situation and environment and how you can use what is in the verse on what is ahead.

PRAYER

Write and pray a prayer to God that includes what you've learned and ask Him to apply the truths of His Word in your life.

CHAPTER 20

"YOU'VE BEEN SO GOOD"

♪

*"You've been so good
And I really wanna thank You, Jesus. . . ."*

READING TIME

As you read Chapter 20: "You've Been So Good" in *Because of Who You Are*, **review**, reflect on, and respond to the text by answering the following questions.

REVIEW, REFLECT, AND RESPOND

How has God been good in your life recently? Have you thanked and worshipped Him enough for this?

_____
_____
_____

Do you believe God has a predetermined direction for your life? What is inhibiting you from following Him to it?

_____
_____
_____

What time do you set aside for your relationship with God? Do you think you could be more intentional and set aside more time? Give some practical steps you can take.

_____
_____
_____
_____

What stands out to you from the lyrics of this song and why? What do these lyrics mean to you?

_____
_____
_____
_____

READINGS: PSALM 34

S:

O:

A:

P:

S.O.A.P.

SCRIPTURE
Write down the scripture that catches your eye (and heart) as you read your Bible each day. Which verses does the Holy Spirit want you to take a second look at?

OBSERVATION
Take time to research and think on the context of the verses you have selected. Who or what are they referring to? Who are they written by?

APPLICATION
What is the application of the selected verse(s)? Think about how the verse applies to your current situation and environment and how you can use what is in the verse on what is ahead.

PRAYER
Write and pray a prayer to God that includes what you've learned and ask Him to apply the truths of His Word in your life.

CHAPTER 21

ASK

♪

"Ask and it will be given to you...."

READING TIME

As you read Chapter 21: "Ask" in *Because of Who You Are*, review, reflect on, and respond to the text by answering the following questions.

REVIEW, REFLECT, AND RESPOND

Is there anything in your life that you want, need, or desire that you're afraid to ask God for? What is it? Why are you hesitant to ask for it?

_____
_____
_____

Do you think God cares about what we want, or only what we need? Why or why not?

_____
_____
_____

What does it mean to desire something according to God's will? Why is this so important?

_____
_____
_____
_____

What stands out to you from the lyrics of this song and why? What do these lyrics mean to you?

_____
_____
_____
_____

READINGS: MATTHEW 7

S:

O:

A:

P:

MARK 11:24

S:

O:

A:

P:

LUKE 11:10-19

S:

O:

A:

P:

S.O.A.P.

SCRIPTURE

Write down the scripture that catches your eye (and heart) as you read your Bible each day. Which verses does the Holy Spirit want you to take a second look at?

OBSERVATION

Take time to research and think on the context of the verses you have selected. Who or what are they referring to? Who are they written by?

APPLICATION

What is the application of the selected verse(s)? Think about how the verse applies to your current situation and environment and how you can use what is in the verse on what is ahead.

PRAYER

Write and pray a prayer to God that includes what you've learned and ask Him to apply the truths of His Word in your life.

CHAPTER 22

COME, HOLY SPIRIT, COME

♪

*"Come, Holy Spirit, Come
And abide within us...."*

READING TIME

As you read Chapter 22: "Come, Holy Spirit, Come" in *Because of Who You Are*, **review**, reflect on, and respond to the text by answering the following questions.

REVIEW, REFLECT, AND RESPOND

What things does the Holy Spirit help us with? How would you define who the Holy Spirit is?

_____
_____
_____

What is the difference between condemnation and conviction? Which does the Holy Spirit use, which does the enemy use, and why?

_____
_____
_____

How often do you invite the Holy Spirit to guide you, grow you, and impart wisdom within you?

_____
_____
_____
_____

What stands out to you from the lyrics of this song and why? What do these lyrics mean to you?

_____
_____
_____
_____

READINGS: JOHN 14

S:

O:

A:

P:

1 JOHN 2:27

S:

O:

A:

P:

ROMANS 8:14

S:

O:

A:

P:

ISAIAH 30:31

S:

O:

A:

P:

♪

EZEKIEL 36:26-27

S:

O:

A:

P:

2 CORINTHIANS 3:17-18

S:

O:

A:

P:

CHAPTER 23

"DECLARATION SONG (DECLARE THE GOODNESS OF OUR GOD)"

♪

*"Jesus is the answer
Declare the goodness of our God...."*

READING TIME

As you read Chapter 21: "Declaration Song (Declare The Goodness Of Our God)" in *Because of Who You Are*, **review, reflect on, and respond to** the text by answering the following questions.

REVIEW, REFLECT, AND RESPOND

How can you "emphatically state" the goodness of God to the world?

_____
_____
_____

How powerful is the tongue and what you speak? What do you need to change most about your speaking habits?

_____
_____
_____
_____

Do you struggle to declare God's goodness when you are going through difficult situations? Why do you think this is? How can you work to change this?

_____
_____
_____
_____

What stands out to you from the lyrics of this song and why? What do these lyrics mean to you?

_____
_____
_____
_____

READINGS: PSALM 8

S:

O:

A:

P:

PSALM 149:5-6

S:

O:

A:

P:

HEBREWS 4:12

S:

O:

A:

P:

LUKE 1:37

S:

O:

A:

P:

♪

JOB 22:28

S:

O:

A:

P:

S.O.A.P.

SCRIPTURE

Write down the scripture that catches your eye (and heart) as you read your Bible each day. Which verses does the Holy Spirit want you to take a second look at?

OBSERVATION

Take time to research and think on the context of the verses you have selected. Who or what are they referring to? Who are they written by?

APPLICATION

What is the application of the selected verse(s)? Think about how the verse applies to your current situation and environment and how you can use what is in the verse on what is ahead.

PRAYER

Write and pray a prayer to God that includes what you've learned and ask Him to apply the truths of His Word in your life.

CHAPTER 24

FIGHT FOR ME

♪

*"I won't worry
I don't have to be afraid
You fight for me..."*

READING TIME

As you read Chapter 24: "Fight For Me" in *Because of Who You Are*, review, reflect on, and respond to the text by answering the following questions.

REVIEW, REFLECT, AND RESPOND

In what ways has God fought for you in your lifetime? Do you think you have seen and recognized all the times He has fought for your best interest? Why or why not?

_____
_____
_____
_____

Have you ever wavered in unbelief as the enemy launched an attack against you? How did this fear or uncertainty penetrate your heart?

_____
_____
_____

What are you going through right now that you need God's help in?

_____
_____
_____

What stands out to you from the lyrics of this song and why? What do these lyrics mean to you?

_____
_____
_____

READINGS: EXODUS 14

S:

O:

A:

P:

2 CORINTHIANS 10:3-4

S:

O:

A:

P:

EPHESIANS 6:10-18

S:

O:

A:

P:

DEUTERONOMY 20:4

S:

O:

A:

P:

CHAPTER 25

"LIFT HIM UP"

♪

"He is worthy to be lifted up...."

READING TIME

As you read Chapter 25: "Lift Him Up" in *Because of Who You Are*, review, reflect on, and respond to the text by answering the following questions.

REVIEW, REFLECT, AND RESPOND

In what ways other than worship can you lift God up through how you act, talk, share His name, etc.?

_____
_____
_____

What do you think your praise shows God? How does it make Him feel and what does it signify?

_____
_____
_____
_____

Do you think praise in the difficult seasons of our lives means more to God than praise in the peaceful seasons? Why or why not?

_____
_____
_____
_____

What stands out to you from the lyrics of this song and why? What do these lyrics mean to you?

_____
_____
_____
_____

READINGS: PSALM 16

S:

O:

A:

P:

HEBREWS 11:6

S:

O:

A:

P:

CHAPTER 26

YOUR LATTER WILL BE GREATER

♪

"The best is yet to come
The best is yet to come...."

READING TIME

As you read Chapter 26: "Your Latter Will Be Greater" in *Because of Who You Are*, **review**, reflect on, and respond to the text by answering the following questions.

REVIEW, REFLECT, AND RESPOND

Where are you now compared to where you were five years ago? Did you think you would be where you are today?

_____
_____
_____
_____

Where do you think God will take you in the next ten years? Are you open to obeying His guidance, no matter where it may take you?

_____
_____
_____
_____

How do you define success in the next ten years of your life—is it a personal accomplishment or kingdom impact? Why?

_____
_____
_____
_____

What stands out to you from the lyrics of this song and why? What do these lyrics mean to you?

_____
_____
_____
_____

READINGS: JOB 18

S:

O:

A:

P:

S.O.A.P.

SCRIPTURE

Write down the scripture that catches your eye (and heart) as you read your Bible each day. Which verses does the Holy Spirit want you to take a second look at?

OBSERVATION

Take time to research and think on the context of the verses you have selected. Who or what are they referring to? Who are they written by?

APPLICATION

What is the application of the selected verse(s)? Think about how the verse applies to your current situation and environment and how you can use what is in the verse on what is ahead.

PRAYER

Write and pray a prayer to God that includes what you've learned and ask Him to apply the truths of His Word in your life.

CHAPTER 27

JESUS IS THE BEST THING (THAT EVER HAPPENED TO ME)

"When I was nothing, He turned me into something...."

READING TIME

As you read Chapter 27: "Jesus Is the Best Thing (That Ever Happened To Me)" in *Because of Who You Are*, review, reflect on, and respond to the text by answering the following questions.

REVIEW, REFLECT, AND RESPOND

What has Jesus Christ done in your life? How do you express this to Him?

_____
_____
_____
_____

How can you better express the gratitude you have for Jesus Christ and what He's done in your life?

_____
_____
_____

What's stopping you from letting others know about the best thing that ever happened to you?

_____
_____
_____

What stands out to you from the lyrics of this song and why? What do these lyrics mean to you?

_____
_____
_____

READINGS: 1 JOHN 4

S:

O:

A:

P:

S.O.A.P.

SCRIPTURE

Write down the scripture that catches your eye (and heart) as you read your Bible each day. Which verses does the Holy Spirit want you to take a second look at?

OBSERVATION

Take time to research and think on the context of the verses you have selected. Who or what are they referring to? Who are they written by?

APPLICATION

What is the application of the selected verse(s)? Think about how the verse applies to your current situation and environment and how you can use what is in the verse on what is ahead.

PRAYER

Write and pray a prayer to God that includes what you've learned and ask Him to apply the truths of His Word in your life.

CHAPTER 28

BEST DAYS

♪

*"He's doing His best work.
Do you know it?
Do you see it?
Just trust Him and believe it. . . ."*

READING TIME

As you read Chapter 28: "Best Days" in *Because of Who You Are*, **review**, reflect on, and respond to the text by answering the following questions.

REVIEW, REFLECT, AND RESPOND

Why is the phrase "seeing is believing" so false when it comes to God? How often does God reveal His plans to us?

_____
_____
_____

What do you feel God is doing in this current season? Where do you believe He is taking you, and what is He teaching you along the way?

_____
_____
_____
_____

How can you better love those around you? What do you need to work on internally so you can better love externally?

_____
_____
_____

What stands out to you from the lyrics of this song and why? What do these lyrics mean to you?

_____
_____
_____
_____

READINGS: ISAIAH 43

S:

O:

A:

P:

HEBREWS 11

S:

O:

A:

P:

CHAPTER 29

"EVERYTHING YOU DO IS A BLESSING

♪

"My joy is a blessing
My test is a blessing
My pain is a blessing. . . ."

READING TIME

As you read Chapter 29: "Everything You Do Is A Blessing" in *Because of Who You Are*, **review**, **reflect on**, and **respond to** the text by answering the following questions.

REVIEW, REFLECT, AND RESPOND

Do you find it challenging to look at your tests, trials, and pain as blessings from the Lord? How are they blessings?

_____
_____
_____

What has God taught you through one of the difficult seasons of your life? Do you think He could have taught you this lesson any other way?

_____
_____
_____

Do you ever try to co-author your story with God? Why or why not? In what ways can you more fully submit to God and His perfect plan for your life?

_____
_____
_____

What stands out to you from the lyrics of this song and why? What do these lyrics mean to you?

_____
_____
_____

READINGS: PSALM 145

S:

O:

A:

P:

S.O.A.P.

SCRIPTURE
Write down the scripture that catches your eye (and heart) as you read your Bible each day. Which verses does the Holy Spirit want you to take a second look at?

OBSERVATION
Take time to research and think on the context of the verses you have selected. Who or what are they referring to? Who are they written by?

APPLICATION
What is the application of the selected verse(s)? Think about how the verse applies to your current situation and environment and how you can use what is in the verse on what is ahead.

PRAYER
Write and pray a prayer to God that includes what you've learned and ask Him to apply the truths of His Word in your life.

CHAPTER 30

GOD IS HERE

♪

*"He is here . . . to break the yoke
and lift the heavy burden."*

READING TIME

As you read Chapter 30: "God Is Here" in *Because of Who You Are*, review, reflect on, and respond to the text by answering the following questions.

REVIEW, REFLECT, AND RESPOND

How do you recognize God's presence? What is God's presence and what does it do?

_____
_____
_____

What burdens do you carry instead of giving them to God?

_____
_____

List some of the reasons you have to worship.

_____
_____
_____

What promise did God speak in Isaiah 10:27 that is available to you today?

_____
_____
_____

What stands out to you from the lyrics of this song and why? What do these lyrics mean to you?

_____
_____
_____

READINGS: ISAIAH 10

S:

O:

A:

P:

LUKE 4:18-19

S:

O:

A:

P:

ISAIAH 27:10

S:

O:

A:

P:

GALATIANS 5:1

S:

O:

A:

P:

MATTHEW 11:28-30

S:

O:

A:

P:

S.O.A.P.

SCRIPTURE

Write down the scripture that catches your eye (and heart) as you read your Bible each day. Which verses does the Holy Spirit want you to take a second look at?

OBSERVATION

Take time to research and think on the context of the verses you have selected. Who or what are they referring to? Who are they written by?

APPLICATION

What is the application of the selected verse(s)? Think about how the verse applies to your current situation and environment and how you can use what is in the verse on what is ahead.

PRAYER

Write and pray a prayer to God that includes what you've learned and ask Him to apply the truths of His Word in your life.

ABOUT THE AUTHOR

Martha Munizzi is a GRAMMY®, Dove®, and Stellar® Award-winning singer-songwriter, pastor, and recording artist, and is considered one of the pioneers of cross-cultural praise and worship music.

Martha has an infectious love for life, a deep love for people, and a zealous love for God's House. Her passion is to help build the church worldwide, see people reach their full potential, and develop and strengthen leaders.

Martha, along with her husband, Dan, and their three children, reside in Orlando, Florida, and are the founders and lead pastors of EpicLife Church in Winter Park, Florida where they both serve as co-pastors.

FOR BOOKING INFO CONTACT US AT:

Martha Munizzi Ministries

P.O. Box 2587

Goldenrod, FL 32733

407-834-5620

booking@marthamunizzi.com

FIND MARTHA AT

🌐 MARTHAMUNIZZI.COM/

📷 WWW.INSTAGRAM.COM/MARTHAMUNIZZI/

📘 WWW.FACEBOOK.COM/MARTHAMUNIZZIFANPAGE

🐦 TWITTER.COM/MARTHAMUNIZZI

▶️ WWW.YOUTUBE.COM/@MARTHAMUNIZZI